# Toys and Games

Sarah Ridley

**W**

**FRANKLIN WATTS**

LONDON•SYDNEY

This edition 2011

First published in 2007
by Franklin Watts

Copyright © Franklin Watts 2007

Franklin Watts
338 Euston Road
London NW1 3BH

Franklin Watts Australia
Level 17/207 Kent Street
Sydney, NSW 2000

Series editor: Sarah Peutrill
Art director: Jonathan Hair
Design: Jane Hawkins

A CIP catalogue record for this book is available from the British Library.

Dewey number: 688.7'2
ISBN: 978 1 4451 0577 2

Picture credits:
The Advertising Archives: 21. © Scalextric.com. Beamish Museum Archive: 14, 24. Colchester Museum Service: 10. Mary Evans Picture Library: 22b, 26b, 27t. 27b. Sally & Richard Greenhill: 6, 13c, 15, 25r. Hulton Archive/ Getty Images: 9, 11t. Manchester Daily Express/Science & Society Picture Library: 3, 20. Museum of Childhood, Edinburgh: 8t, 8b, 13t, 18, 19t. © Nikko-Toys.co.uk: 7br. NMPFT/Kodak Collection/Science & Society Picture Library: 22t. Topfoto: 11c. © Top Trumps. UPP/Topfoto: 19c. © Hasbro.co.uk.

Thanks to the following for kind permission to use their photographs in this publication: Lionel Baker 28; Lucy Bosomworth 17b; David Burrows and family 16b, 25t; Suzanne Greenway 17; Jane Ridley 17t; Nick Ridley cover, endpapers, 12, 16t.

Franklin Watts is a division of Hachette Children's Books, an Hachette UK company.
www.hachette.co.uk

Printed in China

'Boys and girls come out to play,
The moon does shine as bright as day;
Leave your supper and leave your sleep,
And join your playfellows in the street.'

18th Century nursery rhyme

# Contents

# Toys old and new

Some toys and games are thousands of years old. In museums you can see ancient Egyptian toys, such as balls, toy animals, dolls and spinning tops. Many toys were invented during the last 100 years, as you can read in the timeline opposite.

Date: c. 1980

Today many children play on computer and video games. The first games were invented in the 1970s but they have changed a lot since then.

# Timeline

Use this timeline to find out when the toys mentioned in this book were invented.

**1901** Meccano is invented.

**1903** The teddy bear is named after President Teddy Roosevelt of the USA.

**c. 1920** Clockwork Hornby model trains invented, followed by electric train sets in 1925.

**1931** Dinky cars are sold by Hornby.

**1935** Monopoly is sold in Britain.

**1950s** Dolls and many other toys are made in plastic.

**1952** Matchbox cars are first sold.

**1954** Lego is invented.

**1958** The Scalextric racing car toy is invented.

**1960s** Barbie, Sindy and Action Man dolls become popular.

**1970s** The Space Hopper, the skateboard and the Chopper bike get children outside.

**Late 1970s/80s** Video and computer games take off.

**1989** First Nintendo Game Boy is sold.

# Traditional toys

Some toys have hardly changed in hundreds of years. Marbles, spinning tops, toys on wheels, hoops and balls are just some of these toys.

**Date: 1910**

A little girl plays with her parade of animals on wheels. Even the pet guinea-pig is joining in!

**Date: 1910**

Boys watch closely as their friend takes his turn at marbles. Children have made up all sorts of games with marbles over the years.

Two girls use sticks to keep their hoops rolling along in the park.

**Date: 1937**

## Be a history detective

- Do you have marbles? Are your marbles made of glass or plastic?
- The hoops in the photograph are made of wood. What are hoops made of today?

# Teddy bears

Teddy bears were invented over 100 years ago. They are named after US President Teddy Roosevelt. When he saved a bear cub from hunters, newspapers printed the story. Soon toy makers made 'teddy' bears. Children loved them, and still do.

Date: 1914

A girl poses with her teddy bear. It is made from goats' hair fabric and it is stuffed with wood shavings. The bear's eyes are boot buttons, like the ones on her boots.

A girl squeezes the water out of her panda teddy bear, using a mangle. After 1945, many teddy bears were made of washable materials.

**Date: 1961**

**Date: 1970s**

please look after this BEAR. THANK YOU!

In the 1970s and 1980s, some children owned their own Paddington Bear. Paddington was the star of a series of stories by the writer Michael Bond.

# Be a history detective

- How can you tell that the oldest photograph was taken a long time ago? Look at what the girl is wearing.
- What is your teddy bear made of? Look at the label to find out.
- Did your parents own a Paddington Bear?

# Baby toys

Babies like to rattle and roll toys. They enjoy toys they can stack and knock down, and toys that help them to walk. These toys help babies and toddlers to learn new skills.

Date: 1940

Once a toddler is walking, it is great to have something to push, like this wooden horse on wheels.

A baby stacks boxes. These boxes can be stacked up, knocked down or slotted inside each other.

**Date: 1979**

Babies love to shake rattles. Your parents may have had a plastic rattle like this when they were babies.

# Be a history detective

- The stacking boxes are made of card. Have you still got some stacking toys at home? What are they made of?

- Why do you think many modern baby toys are made of plastic?

- What toys did you play with as a baby?

13

# Building toys

In 1901, Frank Hornby created Meccano for his sons. It was a building set with metal strips that could be joined together with nuts and bolts. Lego was invented in 1954. Children could build almost anything out of the colourful bricks.

**Date: 1954**

Boys play with their Meccano model on a doorstep.

Date: c. 1980

It must have taken a while to build this airport from Lego bricks.

## Be a history detective

- How long is it since Meccano was invented?
- Which toy might your parents have played with? And your grandparents?
- Do you play with Lego? Is it the same as the Lego in the photograph?

# In the garden

Ride-in cars, sandpits, tents, swings and slides were around when your grandparents were young. Swingball sets, rollerskates and Space Hoppers were new when your parents were growing up.

**Date: 1942**

The proud owner of this car enjoys his new toy. Look under the car to see how he moves it along.

**Date: 1956**

Children relax outside the tent in their back garden. Your grandparents may have played in a tent like this.

Sisters squeeze into a paddling pool. In the 1960s and 1970s paddling pools were usually smaller than pools today.

**Date: 1968**

**Date: 1979**

Space Hoppers were a new toy in the 1970s. The other children are on stilts.

# Be a history detective

- Ask your parents whether they had a Space Hopper. Have you got a similar toy?
- The car in the oldest photograph is made of metal. What are ride-in toy cars made of today? Do they look the same?

# Dolls

A hundred years ago, dolls' heads were made of china, which broke easily. By the 1950s, most dolls were made of plastic. In the 1960s came Barbie and Sindy, dressed in the latest fashions. Action Man became popular in the 1960s.

Date: 1903

A girl and her doll wear similar clothes. China dolls like this were expensive so girls from poor families played with cheap wooden dolls or homemade rag dolls.

**Date: c. 1948**

A girl takes her doll for a walk. Dolls' prams and pushchairs show us what real baby prams and pushchairs looked like at the time of the photo.

Children could buy different types of Action Man. He could join you in playing whatever adventure you created.

**Date: 1960s**

# Be a history detective

- Ask your mother and grandmother what type of dolls they played with.
- Did your father have an Action Man? How was Action Man different from today's toy?

# Transport toys

Toy trains were invented over 150 years ago, soon after trains themselves. At first, you had to push or pull your toy train along. Then came clockwork trains and finally electric train sets in 1925.

Date: 1961

A boy admires some electric trains at an exhibition. Only wealthy families could afford all of this for their children.

SUPER SPEED 8

NEW

Cars supplied with
'Grand Prix 8' set

Trees illustrated
are not supplied

NO EXTRA CHARGE FOR CREDIT
NO BIG DEPOSIT TO FIND

ONLY
£17·95
38 wks 47p

A

Available in TWO versions
'RALLY CROSS' Set (Illustrated)
and 'GRAND PRIX 8' Set

SCALEXTRIC

Cars are another popular transport toy. Your grandparents may have owned a Dinky car, while your parents probably played with Matchbox cars, or Scalextric racing tracks like this.

# Be a history detective

- What else can you see in the photograph of the train set apart from the trains?

- The 1970s picture was taken for an advert – what clues tell you this?

# Sitting-down games

Toyshops are full of many board games and card games. Some games remain popular for years, such as Snakes and Ladders, which Victorian children played. Others last for just a year or two.

**Date: 1930s**

A family play Monopoly, first sold in Britain in 1935. It is a game about property and money.

Boys play cards on a doorstep. Card games are small and light so you can play them anywhere.

**Date: 1961**

Mr. Dose the Doctor

DOSE

Children have played Happy Families with cards just like these since the 1860s.

Mr. Pots the Painter

POTS

Top Trumps was a new card game in 1977.

Mrs. Dose the Doctor's Wife

DOSE

**Yorkshire**

**Fred TRUEMAN**

| England Caps | 67 |
|---|---|
| No. of Runs | 9231 |
| No. of Wickets | 2304 |
| No. of Centuries | 3 |
| Highest Score | 104 |

**BRITISH CRICKETERS**

TOP TRUMPS

FREE pack offer inside!

**Date: 1980**

Mrs. Dose the Doctor's Wife

# Be a history detective

- Did your parents play Top Trumps with their friends? Have you played Top Trumps?
- What other sitting-down games did your parents play?

# Bicycles and tricycles

One hundred years ago, only the children of wealthy families had bicycles. Other children had fun with homemade go-karts. From the 1930s, many more people could afford a bicycle.

**Date: 1912**

A boy and his sister pose with his tricycle. The three wheels made it easier to ride.

**Date: 1957**

Brothers get set for a ride. Their father made the bikes out of parts from other bikes.

**Date: 1970s**

# Be a history detective

- Do you have a bicycle? Is it like the ones on these pages? How is it different? How is it the same?

In the 1970s, many children longed for a Chopper, with their high handlebars and long seats.

# Playing outside

When your parents and grandparents were young, children played outside much of the time. They made up games, climbed trees, played sport and ran about.

Many children swam in rivers and pools in the summer.

**Date: 1931**

Girls play a skipping game in the street.

**Date: 1946**

Children play cricket in a London street. Many children lived in small houses without gardens or parks close by.

**Date: 1957**

**Date: 1973**

Children enjoy the witch's hat roundabout at a playground.

# Be a history detective

- Ask your parents whether they remember the witch's hat. What do you play on at your local playground?

- How many cars can you count in the cricket photo? Is it safe to play in your street?

# Who is who?

Do you like dressing up? This photograph was taken at a fancy dress party in 1903. The brothers are dressed as Boy Blue, the Knave of Hearts and Dick Turpin (a highwayman). Which one is which? The answer is below.

Date: 1903

Answers: Knave of Hearts – left; Boy Blue – centre; Dick Turpin – right

# Glossary

**Ancient Egyptian** Ancient Egyptian toys were made by people who lived in Egypt between 2,500 and 5,000 years ago.

**Board game** A game which is played with counters, or other playing pieces, on a marked board.

**Boy Blue** The character from the nursery rhyme 'Little Boy Blue come blow your horn'.

**China** Baked white clay used to make dolls' heads 100 years ago.

**Clockwork** Clockwork toys work by turning a key to wind up a spring. As the spring unwinds, it moves wheels and the toy moves.

**Fabric** All kinds of woven materials, such as cotton, linen, silk and nylon.

**Fancy dress** Dressing up in unusual clothes to look like a character from a book or a film, or even from history.

**Highwaymen** People who robbed travellers in Britain around 300 years ago.

**Homemade** Something made by a person, rather than by a machine in a factory.

**Knave of Hearts** A character from the nursery rhyme 'The Queen of Hearts'.

**Mangle** A machine used to squeeze water out of wet clothes, sheets or toys.

**Material** A material is what something is made out of, such as wool, wood or metal.

**Rag doll** A cloth doll made from spare scraps of material.

**Traditional** Something that has been handed down from generation to generation, parent to child, over a long period of time. Traditional toys, such as marbles, hoops and push-along animals, have been made for hundreds, or even thousands, of years.

**Wood shavings** Thin slivers of wood.